No Other To Each Other

The Illumination of Wu Hsin:
Volume Four – No Other To Each Other

Translated by Roy Melvyn
Copyright 2014 Roy Melvyn

Summa Iru Publishing
Boulder, Colorado 80020

Contents

Introduction

With *No Other to Each Other*, Wu Hsin raises the bar. No longer content to speak about the transcendent, he now addresses the immanent, clarifying that it is included in the transcendent.

Very early into *Scroll One: Being Needs No Proof*, Wu Hsin explains:

> *The sage is mysterious.*
> *For such a one, identification has ended.*
> *He has found everything*
> *Where there is nothing.*
> *He sees the essential fullness*
> *Without using his eyes and*
> *Distinguishes between Being and beings*
> *While realizing that there is no need to*
> *Deny the many in order to affirm the One.*
> *His is an unbroken awareness of 'I'.*
> *He lives in a paradoxical locale,*
> *In the absence of anything present and*
> *In the absence of anything absent.*
> *Beyond yet infinitely near,*

Where each is both,

Wholly in the one and wholly in the other,

At the same time;

Where there is no other to each other,

Where the center is everywhere,

Where one plus one equals one

Where emptiness and fullness have no difference and

Where inside and outside,

Where immanence and transcendence are reconciled.

He declares:

I am phenomenal absence,

But the phenomenal manifestation appears as my Self and

I experience the world through Me.

Such a view provides a resolution of the seeming
incompatibility between the One and the many
that has plagued philosophers since the beginnings of
philosophy. It reminds one of the analogy of the fire and its
sparks: the sparks that come off of a fire are both the same as
that fire and different from it. They are the same insofar as
they came from the fire, and are constituted by the same
substance as fire. But they are also distinguishable from the
original fire, as occupying a separate point in space.

That-Which-Is contains both distinction and unity, substance and attribute, universal and particular, whole and parts, all the while maintaining the integrity of Identity immanent within differences.

Scroll Two: The Declaration of Numinous Primacy is essentially an Upanishad. In it, Wu Hsin tackles the impossible, the expression of the ineffable.

He concludes with:

> *That about which nothing can be said,*
> *Wu Hsin has now spoken.*
> *The Final Understanding is*
> *An intuitive apperception that*
> *In every moment of every day,*
> *All that is happening is that*
> *You are looking into a mirror.*
> *There is a singular totality of which*
> *Subjectivity and Objectivity are its twin aspects.*
> *The Subjective aspect looks out*
> *Onto the Objective aspect.*
> *The Transcendent is experiencing*
> *The Immanent via embodiment,*

Experiencing the coincidence of

Difference and sameness,

Fitting together as seamlessly as

The well-made lid fits into its matching box.

Even the sense of being is a

Mere season in the Timeless.

However, at the base,

There always already is a Numinous Individuum.

Thus, on the basis of his meditative direct insight, Wu Hsin celebrates the Absolute or the True Infinite that is the informing principle in all things.

Note to Translation

Material of this nature is not served well by language. It may seem that there are anomalies and contradictions. So, it is important to state that the translation of Wu Hsin's words herein is not purely literal. Instead, it contains an interpretation of what was clearly implied, and this is where the limitation of words is quite evident.

Compounding this problem, I have chosen to incorporate certain words into the translation which may appear to be incongruent relative to the time of Wu Hsin's writing.

The clearest example of this would be my use of the word ego which wasn't to come into being for many of hundreds of years after Wu Hsin's death.

I have done this to best capture the real essence of the intention behind the word. The original Chinese word 个人 (ge ren) means the individual. However, using the individual doesn't capture the sense of separateness that is better conveyed by ego.

The Sanskrit language also provides us with some marvelous insight. In it, the word for mind is manas, which translated literally means that which measures and compares. That says it pretty well. The Sanskrit word for ego is ahamkara; its translation is *I am the doer*. Within the context of Wu Hsin's message, the conveyance of the idea of I am the doer is vitally important. As such, this and other small liberties that I have taken with the translation feel more than reasonable.

RM

Scroll One: Being Needs No Proof

You are not yet satiated from

Your dining on the delicacies of the intellect.

This and your ever increasing body-consciousness

Has made Wu Hsin necessary.

Herein he affirms that there is a natural state,

A harmony in the mutual interaction of all beings

Which arises if not interfered with

By arbitrary external and artificial means.

There is a single source,

With whatever name you choose to assign to it,

From which has emerged

This entire manifestation that is perceived.

It is Being, looked directly in the face,

Unpaired with any thing.

It is in Whom all things have their being, and,

Like a lamp, illuminates them.

It is motionless in all that moves,

The one in what is multiple, and is

Simultaneously interior and exterior to all things.

Your god, your self and the world are therefore

Elements of a Singularity which can be expressed as

"The One as many and the many in One".

Within this manifestation,

You a single object in an infinity of objects.

Nothing more.

The continuity experienced as your self is

Actually Its continuity.

The energy you experience coursing through the body,

The sense of aliveness, is

Its alone.

You are Being.

What are you being as Being?

You are being human.

Where are you being human?

You are being human here.

When are you being human?

You are being human now.

How are you being human?

You are being human through this form.

The eternal Being is that

Into which one must dissolve.

It is that wide expanse which is

Without beginning, end or middle and

Only fools seek to measure It.

Empty your mind and proceed ultimately to

An intuitive knowing beyond sensing and discursive thought.

Penetrate into the interior of yourself so as to

Reach this Source of Being.

Only then can there be a discernment that

You are the all-pervading subtle principle, subtler than space.

The sage is mysterious.

For such a one, identification has ended.

He has found everything

Where there is nothing.

He sees the essential fullness

Without using his eyes and

Distinguishes between Being and beings

While realizing that there is no need to

Deny the many in order to affirm the One.

His is an unbroken awareness of 'I'.

He lives in a paradoxical locale,

In the absence of anything present and

In the absence of anything absent.

Beyond yet infinitely near,

Where each is both,

Wholly in the one and wholly in the other,

At the same time;

Where there is no other to each other,

Where the center is everywhere,

Where one plus one equals one

Where emptiness and fullness have no difference and

Where inside and outside,

Where immanence and transcendence are reconciled.

He declares:

I am phenomenal absence,

But the phenomenal manifestation appears as my Self and

I experience the world through Me.

It is only for those

Who don't understand his singular word that

Wu Hsin has written large volumes.

*****

There is no journey.

When a path is used, a journey ensues.

*****

Wu Hsin cannot force anyone to

Release their grip on their individuality.

When one balances the gains and losses of release,

One knows what to do.

The Self wants nothing,

It has no aspirations.

Wants and aspirations are

The design of the self structure.

Isn't that clear?

Therefore, the search must fall away,

Either from your frustration or from your exhaustion.

Who has ever heard of anyone

Whose search had ended because

They found what they were searching for?

One can meditate for two hours a day for a decade.

But the desired outcome remains elusive and

The conditioning causes the thought

"I'm not doing it the right way".

There is no right way;

There is no way.

All seeking is effort;

There is no effortless seeking.

Some people hear this and

Understand that the grass grows by itself.

The searching is then cancelled.

Others hear it yet continue to search.

For them, the searching has to wear itself out.

In some, it never does.

*****

A jaundiced man sees everything yellowed.

Your world is yours only,

Entirely private.

Nobody can see it as you do or

Experience it as you do.

*****

The drive for worldly fulfillment is

The antithesis of Self Realization.

What is required is Self commitment,

A commitment to Self.

One cannot be committed to

Both Self and the world anymore than
One can go east and west at the same time.

*****

No knife exists that can cut away self-centeredness.

*****

Can you simply stop everything that
You are doing for a single instant and
Submit yourself to the feeling of Being?
You notice that you exist.
Then you notice that you continue to exist.
The investigation is into
What makes up this continuity?
What is when you aren't?
What does one have to do to attain what already is?

*****

You have never been away from perfection.
Any idea of self-improvement is delusional.

Help is of two kinds, the lesser and the greater.

The former is progressive;

It takes you from one point to the next,

With some eventual desired outcome in the future.

Development in intellectual understanding is

A perfect example.

The latter is final,

Eliminating any need for further help like

Removing a child from a burning structure.

*****

Whatever comes has to go.

That which is even before the self

Appears as the self,

Then appears as other-than-self,

Yet all the time, remains the Self.

The Self is always realized.

Wu Hsin merely removes the obstacles.

What is your strategy to undo all of your conditioning?

You must see that anything that

Directs you to a path with

A gradual attainment.

It is no better than chasing after the horizon.

It feeds the belief in becoming;

I must become like this or that.

There are those who refuse to accept this and

Continue on their path until they are exhausted.

At that point of complete exhaustion,

They might possibly be ready.

If you concede that your

View of yourself in the world is only an imagination,

Then it must be clear that any action

You take to rid yourself of the imagination is

Part of the imagination.

The world has the same reality as

The individual who sees it and moves in it.

*****

The Chinese man is often seeking "favorable conditions":

When conditions are favorable, such-and-such occurs.

However, the components that make up

A favorable condition are too numerous to mention.

Why do you, then, believe that

You can create it through your efforts?

Since the Self is both the initiator as well as

The destination, what is it that you feel

You have to do aside from

What is already being done?

*****

You can't think your way to Self recognition.

Believe Wu Hsin,

Thousands and thousands, have tried.

Self recognition is direct and immediate experience.

It is never obtained through any media like

The senses, the mind or the intellect.

It is not a thing to be bound by causes and results.

It is beyond causality altogether.

Any attempt to cause self recognition is meaningless;

The finite and limited cannot cause

The trans-empirical and transcendental experience.

Self recognition is Self abidance,

Nothing more.

If you take Wu Hsin at his word,

Then there cannot be any question remaining such as "How

do I bring about this direct experience?"

Anything you do as doer is like

Watering weeds in order to kill them.

*****

Understanding is granted to those

Who must first recognize the fruitlessness of seeking.

Making tremendous efforts teaches

The futility of effort.

It is like trying to escape from a pit

By digging downward.

Wu Hsin says that no effort is required in

The sense that no effort is required to be aware.

Just relax, don't make an effort to relax.

In that natural relaxation,

What you need to know will present itself.

No one can do it for you just as

No one can eat for you to appease your hunger.

*****

Where is there to go?

There is only a returning to what

One seems to have left.

When the seeming is seen through,

One recognizes that one is where

One has always been.

If it were simply a choice,

Between identifying with

A fragmented, limited self and

Identifying with the unbroken limitlessness,

Surely there would be those who

Readily opt for the latter.

But it is not simply a matter of choice.

Why? Because you are like

The fisherman on the Li River of Guilin.

You control neither the fish nor the water.

You throw your line into the water and

You wait.

*****

Failing to discern your own helplessness,

Your inability to bring about your intended outcome,

You continue the self-centric drive

Onward toward some pre-defined result.

Wu Hsin will admit that there have been

Instances in history where

Enlightenment occurred uninvited.

Yet, in most cases,

It is predicated on a receptivity,

An earnestness,

A desire and an urgency to understand.

In those rare ones,

No further practice as such is mandatory.

However, if the allures of the world hold sway,

Regardless of how profound

The words of Wu Hsin may be,

They will not find their mark.

*****

The purpose of spiritual practice is to be able to

Discern what is not available via practice.

Beauty cannot be acquired via practice

Clarity, likewise, cannot be attained.

Man is the only being that is dissatisfied.

He is the only one wanting to change What-Is.

He wants to manipulate

"There is no enlightenment" into becoming

"There is enlightenment".

He fails to understand that

Enlightenment does not fit into

The concept of cause and effect.

He has failed to make the shift from

A life of getting to one of allowing.

*****

There is no question of doing anything.

There is no one to do anything.

If one holds to the notion that

One is neither the body nor the mind,

What needs to occur

Happens spontaneously through

The body and the mind.

Whatever happens will happen by itself.

There is nothing you, as an entity, can do.

If Wu Hsin's words have taken root,

They will sprout in their time.

*****

Dissatisfaction with worldly preoccupations is

Evidence of the maturation of the homing instinct.

Then, the Self begins to pull oneself to ItSelf.

*****

What effort is required to experience the world?

The Self is so much closer than the world.

What effort can be required to know It?

See that there is nothing to attain.

Do you stop being a man when

You imagine that you are a water buffalo?

He who thinks he is the doer must

Suffer for his doings.

Wu Hsin notes that

Everything happens in its own time.

The one who is ready for the Highest will s

Somehow be made to arrive there.

It will be neither your doing nor Wu Hsin's.

*****

Wu Hsin's only counsel to you is this:

There is nothing objective to what you are.

You have invented a totality to contain you as a part. Refuse

to believe that you are perceivable.

You are that onto which all perceptions come and go.

Seeing this clearly, what's left for you to do?

Your purpose is to be without purpose.

In the absence of purpose,

You can be,

You are authentic because there's

No having to be this or that.

The fisherman cannot control neither

The fish nor the water.

He understands that his role is to come to the water,

Cast his line,

Then watch and wait.

*****

To abide in the highest,

Nothing need be done but imbibe Wu Hsin's words.

Erect an edifice of conviction that

Cannot be demolished.

With Wu Hsin, the formula is not "do this and get that".

Only investigate.

The investigation may be summed up this way:

You know you are.

How do you know it and through what do you know it?

Inspect all the forms of seeming self until

That which is prior to any form of self and becomes obvious.

Proceed along these lines and then return with your questions.

The movement in the direction of

Self knowledge is rare in man.

The two-pronged approach to

The treatment of pain or discomfort is to

Relieve the pain,

Then seek out and treat its source.

In dealing with his self-driven discomfort,

Man consistently stops at the former.

In so doing, he creates a cycle of

Pain-cessation via diversion-another pain.

This has no end.

The drive for permanence,

Permanent happiness,

Permanent security,

Permanent continuity, is what

Takes you away from what is inherent in you.

You have created an imaginary place where

These may be obtained and have labeled it "beyond".

As Wu Hsin has declared so many times before,

There is no going beyond.

There is only returning to "before",

Before this drive for permanence asserted itself.

There is intractable attachment to

Things that are believed to have value.

In that way, attachment to thoughts is due to

The belief that they contain meaning,

Reflect "me", and are necessary for "my survival".

This must be re-examined.

The right view is when

A stranger's coat and "my coat" are of equal value.

*****

There is no difference between

The searching and the self that is searching.

Wu Hsin says make yourself hopeless.

It is hope that

Provides the searching with momentum.

Activities are merely what one 'does',

But not what one 'is'.

What is present is Presence as a whole and

Merely the expression of the Absolute.

Surrender is where all effort has comes to an end,

Where all movement in

The direction of getting something comes to an end.

Unconditional surrender eclipses any spiritual process.

Before one recognizes that this "you" is illusory,

One believes that they can do anything.

Once the illusory nature of "you" is clear,

There is the realization that

There is nothing that you can do.

*****

Let Wu Hsin make this abundantly clear:

When "me" goes, "you" goes with it.

*****

The mind is like a nagging wife.

Why do you continue to listen?

*****

Do not hold Wu Hsin in high regard.

He is merely of an agent of That which is to be realized.

"I Am" is a quality in much the same way as

Sweetness is a quality.

If I am I,

You cannot be I.

If I am I and you are I,

What does I mean?

"I" is not a being but a

Pattern of functioning by the human organism.

When it is made into a person,

It is represented as an entity.

"Who am I?", as entity, cannot be

Answered without memory.

To answer "Who are you?" requires memory.

Who are you in the absence of memory?

The pre-verbal sense "I am" is

The opening act of the play.

In the absence of this sense,

The stage is dark.

When the morning arrives and the last dream ends,

One wakes up: I am,

I am Ling,

I am Ling in the world.

You can't be other than what you are.

As such, surrendering the ideas

You hold about yourself is sufficient.

*****

I think, or there is thinking or there are thoughts.

By what do you know this, how do you know?

Receding further into the background,

You must first know that you are before

You can claim that the world is.

Only then are there thoughts.

By what means do you know that you are?

As long as one remains identified with the body,

One wants to be occupied with actions, because

It is too uncomfortable to acknowledge

One's powerlessness to do anything.

People wrongly believe that

Seeing that "me" is an illusion ends the illusion.

This is only the recognition of the illusion as illusion.

It takes its power away.

Yet, the illusion, the lifestream, continues.

The Self observes a self.

This is key. See that any "me" making any effort only

Produces more "me".

*****

Where the attention goes determines

What is experienced.

A birth-death event, you, has been

Superimposed onto that which always is, I.

In light of that,

Where should attention rest,

On you or on I?

The human problem is a problem of dissatisfaction.

It expresses itself in a variety of modes:

As a longing for meaning,

As the fear of death, or

The sorrow of an unfulfilled life.

At the back of it is

The desire for the infinite.

The purpose of life is the

Overcoming of the human problem.

*****

You only know yourself in relation to other, to objects.

Understand that your body and your mind are

Likewise phenomena that happen to you,

But are not you.

Waking arrives and I am.

Waking goes, dreaming arrives.

Again, I am.

The dreams dissolve and dreamless sleep occurs.

I persist.

The cycles repeat themselves; all the while,

I am.

You are an event,

A creation inside the head,

With beginning, duration and an end,

Represented as a spatiotemporal lifestream.

*****

The individual self can never know lasting peace

Because it always has to defend itself,

To justify itself.

*****

The body is an instrument.

It is yours and not you.

One is always in fear of losing your body.

Yet, it is in that very loss that one gains the most.

The rabbit runs away from

The wolf that is on the hunt.

It is only a body that runs, there is no one who ran.

All notions of a personal self are false.

An action occurred;

At that moment there is only acting, but no actor.

It then follows that any

Life of a personal self is likewise false.

The flower turning to the sun is in

The essential nature of the plant.

The mode of any action of any form,

Its behavior, is inherent in its nature.

There is no entity doing anything; the organism reacts.

Thoughts appear as a necessary function in humans.

The organism does not decide to

Create them any more than it decides to breathe.

They are sourced from

That which sustains and supports the organism.

To believe that you can stop your thoughts,

Presupposes that one initiates them.

This self-deception, this I-am-this-body idea, can die

While the body continues to live.

But there cannot be anyone to bring it about.

The seeming self is an amalgam of

The body and Consciousness, of object and subject.

This seeming self is a series of processes in

Much the same way as is digestion.

What can anyone do to kill their digestion?

Wu Hsin says that all "kill the ego" talk is for novices.

Cut off a man's arm or his leg and

His identity is intact.

But remove his head; then, who is he?

In this fashion,

The removal of the metaphorical head is

The end of identity, which is the herald of Realization.

However, the seeming self does not

Undertake to kill itself.

What dies and what continues?

The movement of air through a flute produces sound. When

that which produces the movement is not there,

Is the sound dead,

Is the flute dead?

The person is a singular point of view,

A particularized consciousness

Surveys a particularized world.

It is a seeming localization of that which is non-local.

Phenomenal presence veils noumenal presence and

Phenomenal absence unveils noumenal presence.

In the absence of the noises of the physical world and

The tumult that is the mental world,

The song of the Self is heard.

*****

Wu Hsin's is the path of abidance, of not moving.

How many can walk such a path?

*****

One is not different from the limitless;

If one still seeks the limitless,

Then the problem may be understood as

One of confusion.

You don't know what you are.

You are only carrying around an idealized version.

When the seeming self is dead,

All thoughts of death are dead.

Believing in the I-am-the-body idea,

Death is feared as being the loss of oneself.

Birth and death pertain to the body only;

But they are superimposed on the Self,

Giving rise to the delusion that

Birth and death relate to the Self.

The Self has no relationships,

Neither with birth nor death.

Wu Hsin affirms this to be true.

*****

It is causeless.

The mind wants to attach causes,

But it is all mere speculation.

One can begin with small steps.

See that there is a difference between

The Self and the apparent self.

Discern that there is the experience of being, I am.

Then, there is the experience of

Being something in particular;

I am tired,

I am hungry,

I am Xin Shu.

Questions will continue until such a time when

The I-am-this-body idea is no longer held.

From the new vantage point, no questions are born. But, the

letting go is not easy because

You have convinced yourself that

The absence of the I-am-this-body idea is

The equivalent of non-being, and that

Invokes great fear.

But not being anything in particular is

Not the same as not being.

The everpresent fear of not-being is real only until

You discern that Being is intemporal.

The paradox of liberation is that it is

Freeing yourself from all that you aren't.

Self Realization is like spontaneous combustion in that

Many of you have travelled great distances

To be with Wu Hsin.

So what he is about to tell you may not be welcome.

All wanting is part of the self-expansion process,

Even the wanting for enlightenment or realization. Doing

anything with

The intended outcome of an attainment

Likewise is part of the self-expansion process.

When one is self-centered,

Everything is framed in relation to the self.

It is a reflexive recoil against

The recognition of its dependency,

The fear that creates distance as

A means of safety.

The inauthentic-I is simply

A reaction to the implied "other" in any moment;

They rise and set together.

In the I-am-this process,

Every "this" is the tool used to substantiate itself.

When one is Self-centered,

Everything is framed as the Self.

Wu Hsin is not this body;

Wu Hsin is that which has embodied.

Being somebody is a distortion of Being embodied.

Taking the former to be the actual

Creates an erroneous referential center and is

The source of confusion.

"I am this body" claiming that

The body is mine makes no sense;

Only Being embodied can rightly claim that

The body is mine.

*****

Transcendence is not a movement

From "this" to "that".

Transcendence is the end of "this".

When you hear a bird's song,
You are clear that the song is not yours.
You don't need to see the bird to know
The song isn't yours.
Therefore, when you perceive a thought,
Why do you assume it to be yours?

*****

Between the Self and the inert physical body,
There arises an 'I' notion, which is
Represented as an individual being.
Intellect has created this division of itself,
A subject and an object via
The action of separative differencing.
You believe that there is somebody
Who is thinking your thoughts,
Somebody who is feeling your feelings.
That is the apparent division.
But it's only apparent, not real.
It is a haunting, a possession by a phantom,
A seeming self.

Wu Hsin's body continues to function in
The absence of a thinker, a planner and a doer.
Wu Hsin is not concerned with either
What exists or with who exists.
To him, it is all entertainment.
His overall attitude is what was considered "mine"
Belongs to That which merely render it on loan.

*****

To speak of the death of the ego is incorrect.
It is a dissolution. Energy is neither created
Nor is it destroyed.
The energy that is the self-centric process
Dissolves and is absorbed back into
The primal field of energy.
Stated differently, the self is subsumed into the Self.

You can never see clearly.

For you to see things as they really are

Requires the removal of this "ash",

Which is the cessation of

One's preoccupation with a seeming self.

*****

Selves are different whereas "I" is only One.

"Other" means outside oneself.

"Other" is the father of fear and alienation.

When one exists in

Presumed independence and separation from

That upon which one ultimately depends,

One fixates on oneself.

One is not conscious of That, and

One automatically withdraws into

A separative and self-protective mode.

"Me" must be seen to be imagination.

If "me" is imagination,

Then all the "of me's", that is,

All the "mine's", are likewise imagination.

When the situation is examined thoroughly,

It is discerned that there is no basis for

Selecting one appearance out of the totality and

Labelling it as 'me'.

As such, there is no "me" who receives enlightenment.

When there is no one home to accept the delivery,

What can be delivered?

The answer cannot be located by thinking.

How many more months, years or decades will it take

Until you see the futility of this approach?

What you are is not conceivable or perceivable.

And you cannot try to deny it by declaring "I am not".

Stop trying to quench this thirst

By drinking the sound of water.

Turn away from thinking.

There is no need for practices per se.

Just ponder the words of Wu Hsin and

Try to grasp their full meaning.

This is sufficient for returning.

Returning means going back to

The source and support of everything and

Resting there.

In that, the misconception that

There never was a thinker, a doer,

A perceiver and an enjoyer simply disappears.

Sooner or later you are bound to discover that

If you really want to end the searching,

You must return the way that you came.

This is what Wu Hsin advises.

It is the way he traveled and he invites you to take it.

The rest is up to you.

You can never find the truth because

This "you" as an entity is a lie.

A lie can never reveal what is true.

It is like living with an ash in your eye.

Your personality or identity,

What is it really?

Is it anything more than "what worked before"

Projected into present circumstances?

During the course of your life,

How many identities have you exchanged?

These identities are little more than

Shirts that you put on and then take off.

Are you merely a shirt?

Or are you something more?

*****

When does identification occur?

Prior to self awareness, there is pure observation

Between the Observing and its instrument.

When the reference "I" is formed,

The derivatives of "I", that is, me and my,

Begin to fall into place.

Every I-am-this or I-am-that

Use I-am as its foundation.

I-am is the ultimate fact;

"What am I?" is the ultimate question.

The life process itself starts with

A lifeless, unfertilized egg and ends,

At what is called death, with

Another lifeless form.

In between these two points,

The Primal Energy has introduced itself.

It has taken a body that was created by the

Fertilization of the egg,

To be its host and its instrument.

The body essentially connects

The Energy to the world.

The resistance to seeing

The true state of affairs may be

Represented by the phrase

"I have to hold onto myself".

The truth of the matter is that

Your sense of yourself is

The domain of your experience.

If you give that up,

It would seem you have been nullified.

In a sense, this is correct.

The conceptual, imagined "you" has been nullified.

The idol that you have prostrated before

Tens of thousands of times has been shattered.

In such nullification,

You discern that what was done was

You took the limitless space that you are and

You stuffed it into a body.

Now freed from all personal constraints,

You relax,

Clear in the knowing that you are all.

Everything that a tiger confronts is a potential meal.

Each and every phenomenon that you confront

Has the potential to bind you, to embroil you, dear Rua.

Let them come, let them go without any attachment.

You will soon come to see that

You are the observing of them and they are not yours.

*****

The self must be view as "it" rather than as "I".

It is the filter through which

The world perception is processed.

There is no "who", only a "what".

Its absence is the absence of delusion.

What you presume to be

The 'I' in the 'I am' is not you.

That "I" is self.

The authentic-I is the ultimate Subjectivity whereas

The inauthentic-I is a usurpation of

The subjectivity by the intellect.

Wu Hsin advises;

Listen to these words with care.

What you take yourself to be is little more than

A pseudo-subjective, experiential,

Linear, temporal stream.

Imbibe this, only.

This is the key.

Do not do not scatter it away

Into the wind like parched rice.

*****

Suffice it to imbibe "You have no shape".

*****

The cessation of thought is the cessation of yourself.

Events are temporal appearances;

They come and go.

The world is an event.

It appears, lasts a while, and then dissolves.

The body and the mind are also events.

The world, your body and your mind all

Happen to you.

With clarity,

This is the immediate, unmediated experience.

When a person is as firmly convinced of

His identity as awareness

As an ordinary person is convinced of

His identity as the body,

He is free.

The seeming self is like

The homeless man who has

Taken up residence in your shed.

He is only there because

You have acquiesced to his being there.

In that sense, you are his accomplice.

Existence without identity is your true nature,

Independent of any and all conditions.

What is it that establishes and maintains

This seeming sense of separation that is

The ground of individual experience?

It is you,

Not "you" as a noun,

But "you" as a verb, an activity.

For the most part, "you" is automatic,

Driven by the root impulse for continuity.

*****

Whatever activities the mind and body are engaged in,

Being neither, how are you affected?

Everything is framed by the triad of the individual,

The world and the deity.

You have to come to see that this is

A framework set up by the separative self-process.

This triad is me, other-than-me, and

Divine-other-than-me.

The real is prior to all these.

*****

Conditioned being can produce only

Conditional beings with conditional identities.

Man tries to define himself by

Attaching himself to things that are not-Self.

All phenomena consisting of

Names and forms are mind only.

All that appear outside are in reality inside.

That which is prior is

Prior to all names and forms,

Prior to any inside and outside.

The creation of the self center takes time

In much the same way as

The creation of a tasty rice dish takes time.

There is the accumulation of ingredients,

There is heating and stirring and finally cooling.

*****

Individuated identification is

The movement away from unity toward

A seeming separate small self.

In this, the body serves as

The anchor for the I am-ness.

After the rise of the thought "I am",

There is the misidentification of the "I" with

The body, the senses, and the mind.

The thought "I am this" follows sequentially

After the first thought.

The senses are the gateways to the waking world.

When they are shut down,

What continues are thoughts and imaginations,

The subtle world revealed in dreams.

Thoughts and imaginations were also

Present during wakefulness but

Now they take the higher seat.

When these too are shut,

What remains is the Perceiving,

Without any content to perceive.

In this state, the bodily functions are

Set low enough so that

The body remains enlivened and does not

Begin to decay.

Perceiving is neutral whereas

The brain in the body is self-centric.

The personal idea, this I, is

The perfume of the self-centricity.

Do you complain about your shadow?
It is there, following around,
But not hindering you in any way.
Step aside from your seeming self and
Treat it in like manner.

*****

The loss of individuality,
The self subsiding in the Self, is the price
One must pay for clarity.

*****

The Self which is of
The nature of Knowing has no sense of 'I'.
Nor does the body which is insentient
Possess a sense of 'I'.
In the taking of
The body as Its instrument for Knowing,
An entanglement occurs.
This entanglement manifests as
Attachment to objects with
The Primal Attachment being attachment to "me".

Wu Hsin reminds you that just a man
Acting as a woman in a stage play does not forget that
He is a man,
All are only yourSelf.
While they may be seemingly separate in appearance,
They are unified in disappearance.

*****

The self is the operations center.
Once the body has received sufficient rest,
This self reasserts itself and
One awakens to another day.
Being the Self requires forgetting "myself".
This is the way of observation,
Understanding and subsequent transcendence wherein
The attention is redirected to the Subject Itself.

*****

Phenomena come and go;
You are their host and they are your guests.
The host continues to be a host
Whether guests arrive or not.

Every day, Wu Hsin urges you not to

Think and act in terms of an entity,

Identified with a body, but you keep doing so.

Can't you see that you are the obstacle?

There is no way other than

Getting out of your own way.

*****

Every individual references him/herself with 'I' and

Then speaks of the possessions of 'I' by using 'my'.

There cannot be 'my' without 'I'.

How many 'authentic-I's' can there be?

This 'authentic-I' is singular existence Itself.

*****

Personhood provides continuity;

The events of life flow from the future into

The present, then to the past.

However, in accepting being a person,

One sacrifices the splendor of the infinite for

The security of the particular.

The person is like

The music produced by the instrument.

A name is merely an address.

What occupies the address is what is important.

When you are alive and conscious,

But no longer self-conscious,

Your days of personhood will have ended.

*****

What you are is simply

The giving up of all involvement with

What you are not.

Reject all that is known and

Extend an invitation to the yet-to-be known.

When all the supports are released,

Then you see that there is no need for support.

The deeper one goes the less one is.

*****

Deathlessness is attained by renunciation of that which dies.

The precursor of real or true knowing is agnosia,

Not knowing.

It is freedom from all conclusions.

Thinking is not the creation of thought;

It is the appearance of thought.

As such, there is no thinker, no one who creates.

There is only that which perceives what appears.

*****

While you are dreaming,

Do you worry that you went to bed hungry?

Each state has a reality that is

Only relative to that state.

In the transcendence of all states,

Nothing exists;

Everything appears to exist.

The self center appears to exist,

Yet it is nothing.

This must be seen clearly.

Just a pinch of salt can pollute a pitcher of milk.

What you are you have always been.

It is only when you become

Something in particular that you are lost.

The self-consciousness fears being without experience.

It uses it as a means to define itself.

Every time you pause in front of a mirror,

Understand what is pausing and why it paused.

Your mind is little more than a drunk monkey.

Treat it as such.

*****

Renouncing evil is not enough.

Goodness too must be renounced.

Then one is impartial.

When this happens, one is able to look at the world and

Appreciate it as if it were a stage performance,

A source of entertainment.

Observe yourself.

Observe your life.

Observe your seeking.

Observe your suffering.

Observe your identification.

Observe your desires.

Observe the totality of the patterns of your existence. Get to know yourself so fully that

You ultimately see through yourself.

If you continue to accept your individuality,

Your seeming progress will be doomed.

Prior to being anything in particular,

Are you or are you not?

To infer one's existence, what evidence is necessary?

That which has been mistaken for "me" is

Essentially Me.

When this is seen clearly, "my" and "mine" fall away.

Once it is seen that any individual is imaginary,

Likewise, the story that refers to its life must be

Conceded to be imaginary.

This so-called life,

This interlude in eternity, does nothing to

Disturb the seamless continuity that is both

Anterior and posterior to it.

It is not an individual who experiences the entire, but

It is the entirety that experiences the entire.

The real 'I' is this entirety of existence,

Without any individuality.

In that sense,

Life lives as each one and

It expresses Itself via

The play of appearance, change, and disappearance.

The person is what Wu Hsin appears to be to other persons.

To himself, he cannot be perceived.

He is not identifiable with any physical or mental state.

Communication through words is difficult.

Wu Hsin's words are heard by

Those believing themselves to have been born.

But does a fish need instruction in swimming?

*****

Wai Gu was a preeminent composer of

Music for the harp.

Yet, he could not teach anyone to play.

Don't assume that

All those with clear sight can teach and

Don't assume that

All those who teach have clear sight.

*****

Attachment is released by seeing through

The falseness of the belief in its value.

The timid leave Wu Hsin, out of fear of extinction, of
The death of identity.

*****

The destruction of self-confidence re-establishes
The reliance on one's source.
The wise call this surrender.

*****

Everyone is looking out from the same place:
Here.
Thus, here becomes everywhere.
Without any reference point,
Here becomes no-where.

*****

The summit lies adjacent to the abyss.

Wu Hsin's prescription has been
Unchanged for decades;
There must be a conscious merging of
What seemed to be other with Source.
Abidance is the only way.

*****

Death is something which cannot affect
That which you are.

*****

The world is an appearance that is
Experienced by a body in the world.
It is the realm of the Energy.
After a time,
All that appeared to exist, vanished.
What did not exist, likewise was not.
What remained after these two is indescribable.

If you insist upon

Removing all the darkness from your room

Before the light can enter,

Yours is an eternal task.

Ignore the darkness and

Get out of the way of the light's entry.

*****

The difference between dreaming and waking is

Like the difference between observing a play and

Performing a role in it.

What is common to them is that

They are each a dramatization.

*****

When one is left without questions,

Then no answers are needed.

*****

After a certain age, one ceases to grow in height

While continuing to grow in concepts.

There is no journey.

You are, as you've always been.

Be where you are and

Know what you are.

This is the best advice Wu Hsin can provide.

Let there be no "me" left to strive for.

*****

Everyone is already enlightened in

The same way that the statue is

Already present in the marble slab.

Both are brought to the forefront via

A clearing away of the unnecessary.

*****

One need not pursue understanding.

The cessation of misunderstanding is sufficient.

All spiritual practice is a subtle resistance to What-Is.

It is the desire to become other than

What one takes oneself to be.

A central problem is that

The intellect is unable to differentiate between

Reality and imagination.

Resistance is always met with resistance

Thereby strengthening the resisted.

Acceptance is never challenged.

Accept that the end of the appearance is

Inherent in every appearance.

No events are lasting, not even I-am.

Life ebbs and flows.

When there is no longer

The compulsion to take a position,

One sees life as it is and the world is

Understood to be a Self proclamation.

*****

The questioning must end.

It doesn't come about by the quality of the answers.

It comes about by seeing that

Asking endless questions isn't the answer.

Wu Hsin is neither this flower pot nor the flowers.

Wu Hsin is that from which they appear.

Equally at home with

Everything and nothing, with

The movable and the immovable,

He is without preference.

*****

Both Wu Hsin and the sculptor

Cut away all that is unnecessary.

The sculptor's task is easier because

He is met with only minimal resistance.

*****

Progress that is not lasting is not progress.

It is the illusion of progress.

Whatever is not lasting is illusory.

Bliss is the absence of phenomena

Wherein the energy is no longer diffused.

It is in which the matrix of

The three natural phases of consciousness:

Waking, dreaming, and deep sleep, are delineated.

*****

The way of total trust is quick,

The way of doubt and investigation is slow.

Yet, all arrive.

*****

Any assignment of form is

An assignment of limitation to

The numinous root of the manifest.

When one asks "Who am I" and receives no answer,

One fails to realize that no answer is the answer.

If you are no thing in particular,

What answer can you expect?

Reality is the underlying,

Supportive condition of all conditions.

It is not an object but rather prior to all objects.

It is What-Is,

Always already the case.

It is what persists after

All concepts have been removed.

The Primary Error of the intellect is that

Embodied Being is mistaken for an embodied being.

"I" as Embodied Being is replaced by

I am an embodied being.

This entire structure is rooted in

The identification with the particular.

Thus, the Universal is masked.

It is an unnecessary addition to

That which is always already the case, to

That Condition from which all conditions arise.

There are great teachers and

There are those that parrot great teachers.

When the great teacher's words are available,

Only a fool would listen to a parrot.

*****

One's fixation on the mental and sensory streams

Misdirects attention away from reality.

*****

When you know what you are,

There is no need for reminders.

The emperor knows he is an emperor whether

He is sitting on a throne or squatting over a toilet. Until you

know what you need to know,

Remind yourself of what Wu Hsin tells you.

*****

Do not make any effort to understand Wu Hsin.

It is only the intellect that can try to understand and

Intellect cannot reach him.

Transiency is the best proof of unreality.

Examination of your reality will

Prompt most of it to dissolve.

Then you will be free in the world because

You have become freed from the world.

*****

The difference between a teacher and a Master is that

One can question a teacher's teaching.

The proper pose with a Master is merely to

Listen and contemplate.

His words are never questioned.

One's work lies in the persistent attempt to cross over

From the verbal to the non-verbal.

*****

Words are no longer true when

One reaches the destination that words point to.

The Self is always present and available at any time.

Take up the study of the Self until

A continuous sense of the Self is in effect.

*****

The first step is to see the fruitlessness of seeking.

All ways that turn you to

Paths, goals, gradual attainments, and

The idea of a promised future that is

Some revolutionary state

Unknown and not presently available are false.

*****

The oil in the lamp fuels the lamp.

When friction is added, it produces flame.

This mind, body and this world are the flame.

When the fuel is removed or exhausted,

This mind, body and world are finished.

One is already sentenced to die.

Only the date is not yet fixed.

Can any doctor make one eternal?

For those seeking immortality,

The first step is to shift the identification from

The conceptual entity to the underlying consciousness.

However, even the consciousness is time-bound and

Likewise must be transcended.

*****

Wu Hsin's verbal sword has the sharpness to

Cut through every erroneous concept.

Yet, understanding can only be imparted as per

The capacity of each listener.

Those are best served who are especially gifted with

The capacity to grow by observing, understanding and

Transcending the self through discrimination.

Even this understanding falls away

Once the destination is reached.

One gets commensurate with what one gives.

Give up a little; get a little.

Give up a lot; get a lot.

Give up everything; gain all.

Wu Hsin places everything into

The hands of those who come.

Nothing is held back.

Each then decides to either

Drop what was placed or to consume it.

*****

Dreams are received;

There is no dreamer.

Thoughts are received;

There is no thinker.

Action is initiated;

There is no actor.

Truth is realized by this processes of elimination.

Empty yourself of all that you think you know,

All your beliefs, and

You will find yourself face to face with Truth.

*****

Each man believes that he is the exception.

Wu Hsin declares that there are no exceptions and

Therefore, there is nothing exceptional.

All occurs within the realm of consciousness, in which

All is possible.

*****

Be at ease.

Have no expectations.

There is nothing to obtain,

Nothing to attain, and

Nothing to retain.

This idea of escaping from illusion is

Part of the illusion.

All attachment is the subtle declaration of "other".

It is the dividing of the Undivided.

Your body is also an object like any other,

So begin to look at it as something separate from you.

Your body is your instrument;

It is not you.

Its death is not your death.

Nothing has greater importance than

Your sense of being, "you are".

When you are not, what is important?

You take yourself to be the director,

But you are merely an actor in

This performance called life.

Can the actor complain that

His character has indigestion?

That which is labeled "unacceptable" is also

A part of the total functioning, and

There is no entity who can pick and choose.

It is only by indoctrination and habit that

You imagine yourself to be

Defined and limited to a body.

Root yourself beyond

The totality of conditional existence;

Only then will you understand how things truly are.

You are like a man who uses an oil lamp

To look for darkness.

Now listen.

The Principle which is in you,

Talks to you through Wu Hsin.

One either believes Wu Hsin or one does not.

If not, why are you here?

*****

When he was young, he was Wu Hsin.

Now he is old, yet he remains Wu Hsin.

The name has not changed while

The form the name refers to has changed.

Name points to form, yet neither is what you are.

All too often,

Physical and spiritual disciplines and rituals are

Prescribed for purification.

Here, none of that happens.

How can the Purest be purified?

Nothing in the world can complete you because

You are already complete.

Therefore, chasing anything in the world is

Merely confusion.

It is like the man who believes that

Hummingbirds hum because

They can't remember the words to the song.

*****

Ask for anything you want.

Wu Hsin has nothing to give.

Presently, there are many clouds that

Obscure your view of the summit.

In their absence, the view is easily gotten.

Wu Hsin places the food in your mouth,

But only you can chew and swallow.

Wu Hsin cannot do it for you.

Regardless of what the world and

One's experiences may seem to be,

That seeming is only

A representation that is determined, conditioned and

Ultimately distorted by the mind.

To see clearly through this,

One must set one's pillow down in

That space prior to mind and sit there.

*****

All seeking is the pursuit of various

Concepts, goals, things, methods, and paths that

Seem to promise release from

Dissatisfaction with What-Is.

*****

No amount of recipe study will

Allow one to know sweetness.

This likewise applies to the reading of scriptures.

In the pursuit of the imaginary,

So much precious time is wasted.

Consider the sad tale of Pu Ti.

He spent twenty years

Trying to hear the sounds blue made.

*****

Ultimately each man must take a stand.

Either he aligns himself with

The short-duration beingness or with

The Eternal.

*****

The perfected man is he

Who is no longer driven to be perfect.

All forms are time bound, space bound.

They are momentary appearances.

You are not apart, nor are

You a part of that which comes and goes,

Which rises and sets.

Those phenomenal constructs which have been

Superimposed notwithstanding,

You are not what you seem to be.

The unity that you seek

Only prevails in disappearance.

In appearance,

Seeming differences and separation are everywhere.

If you seek peace,

Forsake the transitory and

Fall in love with the Not Knowable.

*****

What is taken to be a person, an entity, is

A named form, its processes and behaviors.

It is an expression of the Energy which Itself is

An expression of the Indescribable.

The confusion resides in
Trying to become
What one already is.

*****

That which is beyond the body is non-objective.
It is the Original.

*****

When identified with the body
One requests something to do.
Absent the body identification,
What needs to be done?
Set it down for a time.
Realize the true nature,
Namely that one is only conscious presence
Without any inherent individual aspects.
Then see if there is any need for the body's reclamation.

Before there was knowing, there was not knowing.

In between the two, there can be said to be a bridge-state.

It is that state prior to naming in which

An infant doesn't know it is an infant.

It is after the birth of a form but

Antecedent to the development of intellect and self center.

Some call it the natural state;

Actually, it is the first movement out from

The stateless state of numinosity.

True understanding is obtained only when

Both knowing and not knowing are left behind.

*****

Once it is clear that It is everywhere and non-objective,

The search for It ends and

The seeming individual is then obliged to

Abide in every-moment communion with It.

Beyond communion, all there is is Oneness.

You are in the grip of the Great Illusionist.

Once you understand illusion to be mere illusion,

You can enjoy it for what it is.

You'll discern that it's all a play;

Every act, every scene, takes place in you.

Does the play take place anywhere other than in you?

What is the nature of the experiencer of the play?

In what are the experience, the experiencer, and

The experienced, the world, arising?

The world is like a New Year's celebration in a big city,

Dazzling for a time and then gone.

Never forget that

What is perceived is not doing the perceiving.

All things perceived point back to a center of perceiving.

Beingness can act in the world only with the aid of a body.

Beingness can know the world only with the aid of a body.

As such, all bodies are Its.

Whatever you know is because of

That which facilitates knowing in you.

Direct all investigations toward that.

Being was your first step in the distancing from the Absolute.

Then, your so-called path took you further afield.

It has already taken you too far.

Therefore, you must recede,

You must return.

*****

Exchange a permanent, unchanging identity for

All those identities that change from day to day and

You accept as yours.

They are as discardable as

The dishwater used in cleaning the mid-day meal.

*****

One allocates one's attention to what one values the most.

Those who assign high value to phenomena

Look outward to the world.

Those who value the Self rarely shift their gaze.

They form attachment to the Self

Rather than attachment to objects.

They are slaves to the Self and no longer enslaved by things.

Consciousness is the subtle awareness of

The beginning and ending of all experiences.

It arises in anticipation of

The appearance of something to experience.

In its absence,

All that remains is Noumenon.

*****

When you cannot surrender,

When you cannot go beyond the feeling that

You are confined to yourself and its limited cycle,

Then a nagging sense of incompleteness is your destiny.

One remains embroiled in the constant struggle between

One's drive for personal continuation and the world.

Recognition is possible in the midst of

Any of your habitually fixed states.

It is easy, yet paradoxical.

The paradox is that with the total surrender of the self to Self,

There arises the recognition that Self is all and that

There never was a self to surrender anything.

In order for these words to appear,

This mind with body Wu Hsin has manifest.

It is an in-formed consciousness which has then been named.

*****

Consciousness is a readiness.

It has the power to install sentience.

When it comes in contact with a phenomenon,

There is "consciousness of".

*****

In each state the other two are all but obliterated.

This cycling ends when the lifestream ends.

What is left over is

What has been referred to as the stateless state,

That which is antecedent to all states.

If the individual is not true,

What it perceives and conceives cannot be true.

*****

If you are unwilling to abide by the words of your teacher,

To live them,

Why do you refer to him as teacher?

*****

Pride in one's intellect is merely

An affirmation of the self-referential center

Created by the same intellect.

This self reference point adds to its credentials with

Every action that it labels as "mine".

*****

Wu Hsin says that seeking unique experiences,

Higher experiences, is not the way.

Experiences in themselves are

Merely opportunities to become attached.

There is something fixed on which

The sleep, dream and waking states move and alternate.

There is the continuity of Being in all three states.

This is the Energy.

It lies beyond the perceivable, yet

It serves as its support.

Being is not confined to the body as an individual.

Being is the totality of existence.

It is the fruit of the Energy.

*****

"I am in this body" is not as accurate as

"This body is in me".

*****

Progress is difficult to measure.

If one can now take a form of action which

One was previously incapable of because

The self-strategy one used prevented it,

There is the suggestion of positive movement.

To discuss anything regarding

What happened to you after your arrival is to

Talk about the constructed narrative.

Go back to the source from where

You seem to have come and find out for yourself

What is true and what is mere construction.

Find out what it is in you that remains always,

Which is not coming or going but is

Permanently there.

You were told that you were born,

But from your direct experience,

You might just as well have

Suddenly appeared out of nowhere.

What did you have to do with

The arrival of this sense of presence?

One tends to view life as a process of acquiring, and grasping,

But its highest form is the turning away from

That which tempts one to acquire or grasp and

Turning toward that which is the very source of being.

This is not the source of being this or that, but Being Itself.

*****

There may be numerous paths leading up to the peak,

But only the realized know that they are the peak itself.

*****

One can add to or take away from a construction.

However, in truth, one does not grow

By acquiring something nor is one diminished upon loss.

One remains as one essentially always is.

Only the form of the construction changes.

Wu Hsin wants you to ask yourself:

Did anybody exist prior to me?

When this beingness appeared, then everything else appeared.

Receding, receding, receding, you come to discern that

You don't know anything because your stance is now

Prior to the arising of any thing.

*****

If it can be called a process, it is a simple one.

The student receives the instruction from Wu Hsin.

› He then gives it deep consideration and

Either rejects it or must accept it with

Full confidence and conviction.

He makes it his own by living from it.

You are the support of all that is happening and

You are the observing of all that is happening.

You are the Energy by which

The entire manifestation occurs and by which it is known.

However, you have created

A distorted relationship with the body, taking it to be you.

The right relationship with the body is the same as

The relationship the body has with a spoon.

*****

Free yourself from the intoxication of "I am something".

Then suddenly, unexpectedly,

The feeding of the narrative ceases and

One discerns the entire play.

Free of all manipulative exercises of self,

One is like a mirror to oneself.

Clarity is born.

A man kills a mosquito because it is an annoyance.
How much greater an annoyance is
The idea of a small and limited self?
Why not kill it?

*****

What is this clarity of which Wu Hsin speaks?
It is when the rider of the water buffalo
No longer mistakes himself for the water buffalo.

*****

When you are in a position to observe the mind,
You are standing prior to the mind.

All of creation is Subjectivity in relationship with Its objects,

Consciousness in relationship with phenomena.

It is the recognition of

The transcendent in the immanent and

The immanent in the transcendent.

There is only This.

There is nothing that is not-This.

This always already is.

It need not be searched for.

All searching is mere distraction from This, from What-Is.

The ancients taught that when a man dies,

He becomes his god.

Is this really a becoming or simply

The cessation of the veiling of god?

It is the end of confusion,

An end that need not be brought about solely upon death.

*****

Every want misdirects energy.

As such, it interrupts the constant return of attention to

One's source and support.

Wu Hsin speaks of the restoration of the Primacy,

Of that which was already present at

The time of the birth of the body and

That which will continue on after the body is no more.

*****

When the dreamer awakens,

He loses interest in the dream world.

Likewise, when one awakens here,

Interest in this world is no more and

The life that is lived is one of self-obliviousness,

Without interference.

*****

The misguided must come to see that

Understanding is not a search for experiences

Nor is it a strategic or mental resistance to experiences.

*****

The end of duality is the end of pronouns.

A mirror is needed to see your eyes but

No mirror is required for you to know that you see.

That which assumes the infinity of forms in creation is

ItSelf absolutely formless.

Once one becomes clear about

The scope and vastness of the Self,

One realizes there is no such thing as

"I" as an individual entity.

It is the end of wanting as only individuals have wants.

*****

The time has come to release your preoccupation with

Your level of attainment.

*****

All paths imply movement.

However, there is no need for movement

Once it is clear that you are the destination itself.

Plant this tiny seed of conviction:
"I am neither this body nor this mind".
Water it daily.
Abide there and in due course
It will mature into an unshakable conviction.

*****

What one is is like nakedness.
It is always there.
It is there under the clothing and
It is there in the absence of clothing.
What one is never leaves.
One is mistaken in identifying with
Anything that is not permanent.

There may very well may a time when

You must leave here.

Have no concerns.

Your proximity to Wu Hsin is not the key.

Your proximity to Wu Hsin's words is the key.

Take them with you,

Insert them in your hearts, and you cannot fail.

*****

You are like a flame, dependent on the fuel.

The arrival of the Energy brings with it

The media of time and space.

It is the primary cause,

The prerequisite for anything else to be.

*****

The statement "All is divine" includes each one of you.

That which is divine never excludes.

When you see the world,

You see the divine.

There is no seeing the divine, apart from the world.

When one is involved in the world,

One cannot immunize oneself against the world.

Even the Emperor gets indigestion.

*****

Wu Hsin clarifies:

The waking state is a continuity whereas

Dreams are discontinuous.

However, the waking state too is a discontinuity in

The triad of waking, dream and dreamless sleep.

*****

Stop your complaining.

The reason that there is no realization is that

You are trying to realize

Without giving up the bodily identification.

Man's senses report duality.

Whatever is seen is only

The vision of the Self objectified.

*****

One has taken the physical construct

Which has been created to act as an emissary for the Energy,

To be oneself and

Accepts that as oneself.

However, the Energy is not perceivable.

Therefore, it must never be

Mistaken for the person, which is perceivable.

*****

The same power that ripens the fruits,

Ripens you too.

What does the fruit do in order to ripen?

Attend to that which is essential;

This is your sole work.

Clear sight is the re-cognition of the Priormost,

The essential nature of things,

Wherein all is seen as an aspect of

That by which all is seen.

*****

The light is never affected by the shadows it creates.

All paths, methods, forms of seeking, beliefs, and religions

Grow out of a subtle dissatisfaction with the known.

Wu Hsin's sole purpose is to undermine

All seekings, all paths and all methods.

Without putting in any effort,

The experience of the world happens.

By what magic does this occur?

There seems to be an external world that is objective,

But in your absence as sentience, as Subjectivity, where is it?

Since it appears in you,

Your absence means its absence.

The world is seen only after "I am" is declared.

This body you have claimed and

The world that it appears in are a singular existence.

Understand yourself to be the Energy,

The Primary Kinetic Structure underpinning all of existence.

There is consciousness.

The apparent entity is within that consciousness.

When consciousness reasserts its primacy over appearances,

That is true understanding.

This awakening to one's non-objective existence produces

A right relationship to experience.

*****

You, as a concept, is constantly reinforced.

It is like driving a nail into a wall.

Once the nail is in completely,

It is difficult to dislodge.

*****

There can be no meeting the Self.

To meet the Self requires one be separate from It and

That is not the case.

Do not misunderstand the directive to study.

Study is nothing more than

The continuous consideration of Wu Hsin's argument.

An ordinary man can understand something if

It is explained a few times.

If he repeats it twenty times,

It becomes habitual.

If he repeats it a thousand times,

It becomes inherent in him.

You are unchanging and continuous,

Cycling through the three states which are

Constantly changing and therefore transient.

You are always.

Any attempt to describe what you essentially are

Must invariably be colored by imagination.

You are literally unimaginable.

However, there exists a fundamental tension between

The self-referential processes which

Demand identification for validation and

The essential fact that

What you truly are is not perceivable, and

Therefore cannot support identification.

*****

There can be nothing called 'mine' where

'I-am-this' is not present.

The primary hurdle in all teachings

Lies in experientially realizing

What has been intellectually understood.

Wu Hsin provides the accessible

But it is yet to be accessed.

It is only when one pauses the habitual thought process and

Impartially observes, that a subtle succinctness

Arises to allow the eyes to fully open.

Whatever was viewed to be unachievable,

Becomes achieved.

*****

Whenever you put in effort, it is body-based.

If the body is not yours, how can the effort be yours?

The effort required for the awakening or realization is of

The same magnitude as

The effort required to awaken from sleep.

Make the transition from trying harder

To trying easier to not trying.

Detachment towards objects is brought about by
Understanding their true nature.
One doesn't salivate at the sight of a wooden apple.

*****

Even an emperor is no match for
A man with no dissatisfaction.

*****

To Wu Hsin you are like newly born birds,
Craning their necks with mouths wide open,
Waiting for Wu Hsin to
Drop a bit of food down their anxious throats.
There is nothing to give, nothing to receive.
It is all already always present if you but avail yourselves of it.
It is enough to understand Wu Hsin's core meaning.
Once you abide in the meaning,
Where is the need for practice?

Reality exists independent of its human constructions.

*****

There is Consciousness.

When there is an object in Consciousness,

One will experience it as knowledge of objects.

When there is no object,

It is experienced as objectless knowledge.

It is Pure Consciousness and it is prior.

It is the readiness to touch the yet-to-be-known.

*****

Even in utter darkness when he cannot see his hand,

Is there any doubt that the hand is there?

It is the same with Being.

So long as self centric seeking exists,

Clear view is not possible.

*****

Thought is not the problem.

"My thoughts" is the problem.

Do your neighbor's thoughts trouble you?

In every act and every thought,

The essential question is:

"What is thinking, what is acting?"

*****

As the salt is inherent in ocean water,

Similarly, in the inert body, the Energy appears.

This Beingness is of two main states,

The experiential and the non-experiential.

The experiential can then be

Further divided into waking and dreaming.

The radical point of view is not

One of seeking, sequentially through experiences,

But by penetrating prior to any movement, What-Is.

This understanding, when it occurs,

Will not be your enlightenment,

Because when it occurs there is no one left.

Yet, there still is an apparent individual.

He remains ordinary,

But he now lives from the point of view of the Self,

As the Self.

*****

Not-Self only exists in duality.

In the unitary view, all is oneness.

*****

The mind is the first projection of Consciousness.

It is the wall onto which all the shadows appear.

Silver has no shape,

Yet silver can take shape.

In the same way, the Shapeless takes numerous shapes.

This spectacle appearing as

The world is an infinite number of Its form.

*****

When there is neither memory of Self

Nor forgetfulness of Self,

There is just being oneSelf, this is illumination,

That which is beyond description,

The witness of consciousness.

When water is turned into ice,

It continues to be water, does it not?

Likewise, one is never not oneSelf.

*****

Coming to Wu Hsin for techniques, methods or experiences is

A form of self-defense.

It is the defense of one's search,

Seeking sustenance for the search.

The natural state of consciousness is not "me."

It is not in any sense

The feeling of being apart,

Observing things apart,

Any obsession with self or any feeling of being separate.

Don't be a fool, Chongqin.

Until you forget yourself,

How will you know anything?

*****

When growth stops, dissolution begins.

The root cause of death is nothing other than birth.

*****

What is your work here with Wu Hsin?

It lies in breaking the habit of

When looking at the lesser, the greater is forgotten.

The preoccupation with objects results in

Forgetting that which is Subjective.

The remedy is the religion of Wu Hsin.

Wu Hsin has no need for the light of a lamp to see the sun.

Being proves its own existence

By witnessing everything other than itself.

*****

The experiential state comes uninvited, unsolicited.

The waking world appears,

The dream world appears.

To gain knowledge of material objects,

A material form is required.

To gain knowledge of imaginary objects,

An imaginary form is required.

All the while, the observer of the play is not in the play.

The observer is in the audience;

The observer is the audience.

*****

Understanding arrives at different paces for different people.

Just as a bucket with a small hole in the base

Lets water move through it slower than

A bucket with a larger hole,

Likewise, clarity dawns in its own time.

The illuminations gained by trance states are

Always temporary.

As with any temporary phenomena,

They are not to be embraced.

*****

One must step out of the drama of the so-called personal life.

The paradox is that such stepping out is

Part of the drama.

*****

What power has Wu Hsin?

Wu Hsin is powerless to do anything other than to

Lead you to the portal,

Invite your entrance,

Bow and depart.

How can Wu Hsin describe the Essential?

To the extent that the experience is one of a unity,

It is not dual.

It swallows individuality.

And yet it displays plurality.

How to know It?

Sink yourselves in the universal consciousness and

Make yourselves co-extensive with all that is.

*****

To feel that you are an individual is illusory.

The one who wants to break free of it is also illusory.

*****

Thirty years of higher experiences may occupy a fool,

But only an awakened man sees clearly.

*****

Find the actor who is behind the acting,

The thinker behind the thought,

The one who wills behind the act of willing.

Inside nothing, outside everything.

Oneness described.

*****

When a mind changes,

The world changes.

Wherever the mind goes,

Consciousness is already there.

This eternal witness of the transient is unchanging, unmoving.

*****

When the mind wanders, don't follow it.

Spend less time on self understanding and

More time on Self understanding,

The shifting of the center of attention from

The inauthentic to the Self, from

The individual to the Supreme.

This is undermining the self.

As without water there is no ice,

Without the Energy, nothing is.

*****

There is no need to reject multiplicity and variety.

Only see that as related to the Ultimate,

"Not-this" cannot apply to any object.

*****

Mine-ness converts everyone into a watchman.

*****

Can you keep quiet long enough so that

A listening to Being may occur?

Listen and awaken.

Unless one becomes steady within oneself,

Leaving behind that which seems external,

One is as good as deaf.

Not a thing exists without there already in place

That which perceives it.

Before the world was,

Consciousness was awaiting it.

In consciousness it appeared,

In it lingered and

In it will ultimately dissolve.

*****

The escape from the vortex is through the center.

*****

The experiences themselves are not what it is pivotal,

Nor are your reactions to the experiences,

Nor are your questions about them,

Nor is their content or their interpretation.

Understanding is the point of your time here.

The Seeing is eternal

Whereas the seen are temporal.

You are before the mind is.

You have to be there before the mind appears.

This existence is all-pervading,

Both in inanimate objects such as rocks and in the animated.

*****

Only when you leave everything behind,

Can you find the Beginningless.

*****

Be still.

Stillness is your nature.

From stillness, the body moves.

From stillness the mind moves.

To stillness, they both return.

Just be aware, without any striving for a goal.

Dwell serenely in your inherent formlessness.

What is there to practice?

Does the towel exert effort in soaking up the water?

There is a room in which there is a wife, a sister,

A daughter, and an aunt.

Can you tell Wu Hsin how many women are there?

Remove all the names and understand.

*****

There is nothing to attain,

Only something to be realized.

It is not the case that there are bonds to be broken,

Only that one realizes that

There never were any bonds to be broken.

*****

All becoming is delusion.

Does Spring become Summer?

Does incense become ash?

*****

One identifies with limitation and

Then wails that he is limited.

Wu Hsin sees the joke, do you?

One creates one's own jail.

The cell door opens when the identification ceases.

*****

Everything must go in order for It to be realized.

This includes the aspiration for the realization of It.

*****

To see anything clearly, illumination is necessary.

Only an illuminated consciousness can dissolve

The seeming self,

This product of the urge for survival

Filtered through the intellect.

What is this Potentiality?

It is like the dormancy of fire in a tree.

*****

Letting go of everything that was previously clung to,

One discerns that everything which in fact

One always was.

It is only in the suspension of

Your awareness of yourself that

There appears that awareness of the One Self.

Of that which is

All-pervasive, unobstructed and unobstructing,

Pure, formless, unattainable, stable,

Empty, unattached, impartial,

Beyond the distinctions between void and non-void and

Between inner and outer.

Words, what is the use of them?

Either one is not ready, in which case

The so-called word is no more than empty or else

One is ready and then

Words are unnecessary and even

The sound of thunder will suffice.

*****

Identity is built after the arrival of

The sense of other.

*****

Where does one draw the line between I and it?

A common error is equating Being with

The pre-verbal sense of being.

The absence of the latter is mistaken for

The absence of the former.

The feeling of the sense of being is

The primordial experience.

Prior to it is the non-experiential,

The Absolute which has no qualities.

*****

Consciousness is like the public well in the town center.

Everyone goes to use it, yet

No one claims the waters to be "mine".

*****

How can one speak of the experience of timelessness?

Even the experience of timelessness occurs in time.

There is really no such thing as non-self, but

Wu Hsin presents non-self as

A concept to enable understanding.

*****

Self is the Energy, the essence of Awareness.

In its absence, all objects are inanimate and unknowable.

Prior to It is Noumenon,

The original impulse.

*****

Salt dissolved in water

Continues to exist as a quality, taste and

Its existence is known by such taste.

Similarly Being, though not recognized by the intellect,

Can still be realized in a different way,

Via direct intuition.

The transcendent and the imminent seem to be a pairing.

In the ultimate realization,

They are shown to be a non-dual reciprocity.

*****

There is no searching for the Self.

As Self cannot be found by thoughts,

One cannot think about it.

The Self is invisible and cannot be felt.

It is formless and colorless.

While permeating everything,

It is different from what is created.

It is the doer of every action.

As the sun dries the clothes without

Coming to dry the clothes,

So It is.

*****

Reality has to be taken from wherever it comes.

It possesses, one does not possess It.

One who is serious gives up all idle chatter and distractions,

Devoting oneself for all time to silence.

Enter into oneself to the place where

There is nothing and

Take care that nothing enters there.

*****

If a healthy man asks his physician to heal his malady,

Is he not a fool?

Why ask Wu Hsin for aid to become what one already is?

*****

Value only what is seen when the eyes are closed.

*****

There are too many who mistake

The landings on the staircase for the rooftop.

Shun the charlatans.

One can transmit only what one has oneself.

No one can awaken a sleeper if one is asleep oneself.

There is no self inside.

It therefore makes no sense to talk about

The world as being outside.

*****

Shift the attention away from thinking, feeling, and doing.

Affix it to Being.

*****

So long as you think of a self that

Has to be transcended or annihilated,

You continue in your role as

Accomplice to its feeding!

*****

The eyes will see only if there is something to be seen.

If there is nothing to be seen,

The eyes will still exist.

Likewise, consciousness is there whether or not

There is anything to be conscious of.

Only the wise let whatever happens, happen.

They let whatever has to go, go.

With unswerving identity with the One,

What does any of it matter?

They are now face to face with the faceless Self.

*****

That which is yours is not you.

It is not the body that observes the body.

Can a corpse observe its funeral?

*****

The awareness that seemed to be observing the world

Must be realized to be one with it.

It is a singular of which the plural is unknown.

*****

To know yourSelf, you must

Have yourSelf in mind all the time,

Until the secret is revealed.

The empirical knowledge of external phenomena and

The internalized state of the introverted mind merge,

Resulting in Fullness.

They two are only aspects of one Reality.

There is no time when Full is not full.

This is why It is referred to as the Always Already.

What can be added to Fullness?

Hence, therein, one plus one equals one.

*****

Prior to any meditation,

What is it that is already present?

In recognition of that,

The need for meditation drops off.

*****

"You" and "me" is in reference to the bodies.

"I" is the highest.

I am before the thought "I am".

This is Being.

This is Consciousness.

This is Fullness and Completeness.

This, I am.

*****

Nothing exists without a spectator.

As such, you are the support of all.

In your absence, nothing is.

*****

The shortest path to the top of the mountain

Abandons "me" and "mine" at the base.

At the instant of

The emanation of the world from Noumenon,

The Energy, time, space, and phenomena all came into being.

In lightning fast succession,

First the Energy is sired,

Then the mind appears,

Then the body, and

Finally, the world appears.

Exactly when did the world appear?

When did you perceive it?

*****

Do not concern yourself with your future.

It is already contained in you.

Forests, caves and mountaintops are like cities to
One who continues to think.
With cessation, one gains clear perception of what is,
A selflessness, and the freedom from
The drive to acquire or to reject.
One sees only the Self,
One sees the world as an emanation from the Self and
One sees such world as mySelf.

*****

In the end, there must be tremendous effort so as
Not to cling to any effort.

*****

The Absolute projects or emanates
A world as an evolving continuum
Yet remains the ever-present source of
Both the experiencer and its experience.

The foundation and support of all that appears is
'Here and now I am'.
For as long as one considers oneself to be a phenomenon, a
A named shape,
One will continue to be influenced by phenomena.
When one is no longer taken to be a phenomenon,
One is impervious.

*****

It is the nature of the seen to cause one
To forget that which sees.

*****

Solitude does not depend on externals.
It is inner stillness.

*****

Beingness expresses with the sequence "I am",
"I am this",
"I am this in the world".
Both Subject and object are now fully situated.

Being is the most obvious.

Yet it is so easily overlooked.

Its recognition neutralizes all paths and methods.

Only if the way is external, directions are possible.

Does a holy place go on a pilgrimage?

*****

All phenomena require attention for existence.

The ignored have no being.

*****

The state of Wu Hsin is not that of trance.

He observes the waxing and waning of the world

While abiding in unshakable serenity and fullness.

One must discover for oneself

The I that is constant, the same,

Unaffected by waking, dreaming, and sleeping.

*****

When you are confident in its effectiveness,

You take the medicine.

Wu Hsin's medicine is available to all;

Only the confident take it.

*****

The one who distinguishes the within from

Oneself who seeks the within, is

Not yet within.

*****

Come to know oneself in relation to oneself,

Not in relation to other things.

See that everything is inter-related.

Nothing has its own self-contained existence.

The center is everywhere.

Consciousness is the First Movement.

It is the bridge between the potential and the actual,

Between Noumenal Being and

Phenomenal existence and experience.

*****

You don't have any goal,

You finally perceive how close you are to it.

Awakening is the awakening to

That which is beyond waking, dreaming, and sleeping.

*****

That which is there before the beginning and

After the ending of everything is

The causeless cause of everything.

*****

Even when there is nothing to be observed,

You are there in the readiness to observe.

Renunciation is simply to discard what is not useful.

When the crystal is placed against a red flower,

It seems to become red.

The crystal is not enhanced in any way.

*****

At the time of birth,

The power for the realization is the same for all.

Most squander such power by directing it toward

A life of service to the stomach, the genitalia and

The sense of self.

*****

The beginning and end of life is

A small event that happens in

That which is permanent.

There is no one it happens to.

It Moves,

It Knows.

These are Its twin aspects in the same way as

Heat and light are two attributes of the sun.

*****

It begins where concepts end.

One may name it Consciousness, the Witness, or the Doer.

This is unimportant.

What is important is to understand that

When It vanishes, everything vanishes.

The world exists only as long as it is perceived.

*****

There is confusion,

Like seeking fireflies in bright sunlight or

Like asking where a circle starts or

Like catching smoke.

The end of delusion is the end of confusion;

Two names within a singular stance.

You come to Wu Hsin and are told that
You are neither the body nor the mind.
Yet, you refuse to believe.
So why do you come?

*****

One stands outside of the field of consciousness.
One is neither the field nor its contents.
One is the Self.
Why not abide as the Self?
This is simply the non-identification

*****

You are not the body,
You are the Energy in the body, and
This Energy is always free.

Discriminate between the words of the sage and

The words of the philosopher.

The latter speaks profoundly of Guilin

But has never been there

Whereas, to the former, Guilin is his home.

*****

The Essence is self-luminous;

No light or other instrument is required to see It.

Unperceivable and indescribable,

Not available to either

The intellect or the senses,

It is the light behind consciousness,

Prior to consciousness wherein

Consciousness is like sunlight, yet not the sun.

Hearing Its soundless sound requires nothing,

Least of all practice.

Ideas support the world of ideas.

The words of Wu Hsin are to awaken,

Not to instruct.

There is nothing new here.

Although the words may be different,

The scaffolding is thousands of years old.

*****

The seeker's dilemma lies in the belief that

The success of his search depends wholly on

The efforts that he makes and

The determination with which he makes the efforts.

This gives credence to his confusion.

*****

The only obstacle is believing that

There is someone to surmount the obstacle.

So long as you seek you own ends while pretending to seek It,

You will never find It.

The seeking ends at the same time as

The individual ends.

Identity, individuality, and uniqueness are

The aspects of I-am-this.

The only path to follow is the one by which you came.

Overcoming all conditioning,

Retrace I-am-this back through I-am to I.

*****

The thread is ignored,

Yet in its absence, there is no cloth.

First communion,

Then immersion,

Last absorption

*****

The Energy is just as much in the making of a good soup as

It is in the sun's shining.

Any seeking presupposes that

The sought is something different from the seeker.

This calls out for re-examination.

*****

There is no need to preoccupy oneself with

"What should I be doing, Master?"

Wu Hsin reminds you that life goes on as it is supposed to,

Regardless of what any seeming individual thinks he is doing.

What does the lake do to reflect the moon?

*****

The world disappears into and arises out of

The One that leaves no signs.

It is experienced in one of two ways,

As a seeming or as it is.

All intention is the attempt to manipulate What-Is.

When one sees all things in the Self and

The Self in all things,

The urge to manipulate dissolves.

*****

As a water-buffalo-pulled plough is of no use to

A farm ripe with rice,

Likewise, all practices are worthless to

One who discerns that there is nothing to attain.

*****

Out of the not-even-one,

One emerges.

From one then two, then many.

In the same way that one is the source of two,

I is the source of I-am.

There is Subjectivity,

There is the realm of phenomena and

There is the conceptual line that divides the two.

When the three are apperceived as a unity,

The problem is resolved.

*****

To whom does the unawakened state belong?

Only to the seeming one who seems to be unawakened.

*****

There is nothing but being,

In all its fullness,

In the multiple forms in which it appears.

Regardless of appearance,

The forest emerges from a singular root.

Thus, the world is understood as

The manifestation of the dynamic aspect of the Energy, and

Should be celebrated and experienced.

This body owes everything to its association with its Source.

Disassociated, what can it accomplish?

*****

Let things take their own course,

What does it matter to the Energy?

Whatever happens,

Whatever is gained or lost,

It has no concern.

*****

As the water held by a container

Continues to be water and only water

Regardless of the shape of the container,

The Energy is antecedent,

Regardless of the shape it assumes.

You are not your experience.

Experience is what comes to you, what arises in you.

You are not unhappy;

Unhappiness arises.

You are not thinking;

Thought arises.

Through this, Wu Hsin clarifies that
It is only the Energy that is experiencing.

*****

When "I" do not exist,
The question of "mine" does not arise.

*****

 All happiness is predicated on
A harmonious relationship with other-than-I.

*****

All actions are reactions in the body-mind organism to
An impulse, a movement in the Energy.

*****

The seeming self is a thief, appropriating that which
Belongs to the Self and making it its own.

You have come to Wu Hsin looking for peace, Xiu Xi, and
Wu Hsin shall provide it.
Stabilize at that point where you started to be;
This is where peace resides.

*****

When one looks in the external,
All that one finds is external.
Interest in any experience distracts one from
That which is antecedent to all experience.
The temporary never leads to the permanent.

*****

You are wearing the robe but you are not the robe.
You may say that the body is yours,
But it is not you.
There is no individual except through
Identification with the body.
When nothing is, you still are.

Ego is both real and unreal.

It is real in the way that an echo is real and

It is unreal as an independent entity.

This sets up the Primary Confusion,

That there is a you experiencing

A world outside of you.

What seems to be you is really

A production by a multitude of separate processes

Of which this "you" is not aware and

Over which you exert no intentional control.

*****

What is seeking other than

An illusory desire on the part of

An illusory individual to achieve

An illusory goal?

*****

The infinite variety of conditions depends on

The individual's infinite ability to take on conditioning.

Wu Hsin's stance is that
There is no time when he did not exist.
Where he did not exist, there was no time.

*****

Consciousness is both the eternal seeing and
The empirical object.
As such, everything is of Consciousness and
As Consciousness.

*****

With the letting go of seeming limitation,
Fullness is realized.

*****

A man can drown even in shallow water.
Just a bit of confusion is sufficient to foil one's clarity.

The All does not create;

Nothing can be added to everything.

The All projects Itself as phenomena,

Its objective expression.

This results in a seeming distinction between

The Absolute and the conditional.

*****

Those who have apperceived that

The Self is neither bound nor liberated,

Are themselves truly liberated.

*****

Every moment provides another choice

Between detachment and involvement.

Caught up in the obsession with

The endless stream of his own thought,

Man remains ensnared.

Just as water is present between two successive waves,

So too is the Energy present between

The appearance and disappearance of every phenomenon.

*****

The Self is of no use to the worldly.

*****

In darkness, all objects can be seen with

The help of a lamp.

Due to the light of the sun,

All objects including the lamp are visible.

It is Consciousness that facilitates the seeing of

Not only all objects and the lamp, but also the sun.

*****

The sage always lives in a spontaneous and natural state,

Whereas the individual is always affected by

The world and lives from a particularized stance.

The flame will last as long as the fuel oil is there.

Only fools speak of liberating or awakening for the flame.

How much time they waste punching fire.

*****

Understanding is not a matter of time.

It occurs outside of time in an eternal instant.

*****

It is the nature of the Energy to express itself;

Thus, worlds are born.

*****

Like the sun and its rays,

The Supreme radiates Itself in various forms.

For as long as you have not penetrated to that
Innermost source from which diversity itself originates,
You are merely cherishing external idols which
You have created.
For the one who has seen through the veiling,
Petitionary prayer is no longer possible.

*****

The world is an appearance.
In that sense, it is and
Yet it is not.

*****

Realization is the metaphysical apprehension of
The Absolute as an eternally self-realized fact and not
A spiritual attainment or add-on.

The cessation of confusion and seeming embodiedness is not

Brought about by practice,

But only by direct intuition.

*****

Wu Hsin may share his home with mice,

But he does nothing to feed them.

Likewise, unfed thoughts die out.

In the same way that fuel makes a fire burn vigorously,

Fueled thoughts go on unending.

*****

When one starts to think about It,

One has already made the first mistake.

That Which Is declares Itself via

The human form as 'I am'.

Whatever is then perceived is

Perceived through Its instrument, "me".

Since nothing truly is until it is observed,

Consciousness must be part of the fabric of reality;

In fact, it is the thread from which

Such fabric is made.

*****

Wu Hsin is here to chase away the dark with a fiery torch.

With him, one undertakes the pilgrimage from

The many to the One culminating in the elimination of

The seeming sense of finiteness and fragmentariness.

Therein, the boundaries of any self,

Which distinguish a 'me' from others,

Dissolves once it is realized to be not a thing

Separate from the world but

A referral point

From which the world is experienced.

Man is constantly taking the evidence of his senses to be

The seal of reality.

Don't you know that the senses mislead?

One takes oneself to be both acting and acted upon.

However, this is a distortion of the experiencing structure.

If the structure is distorted,

The experience must likewise be distorted.

It results in confusion, like asking

"Where does the sun go at night?" or

Believing that a buffalo reflected in a mirror

Affects the weight of the mirror.

*****

There are not multiple objects with multiple existences.

There is existent continuity and it is one.

All apparent illusions are real cognitions.

The finite is an appearance in the sense that

It is a partial expression of the Infinite.

It is this Infinite that contains

An infinity of finites.

With the transcendence of the limitations of finitude,

The finite unites with the Absolute.

You are not the body.

You are being conscious presence.

Accept it.

Then forget it.

*****

Listen to Wu Hsin's words but expect no benefit.

A benefit requires someone to benefit and

There is none as such.

*****

The prism of consciousness creates the trinity of Experiencing,

The instrument of Experiencing and the experienced.

View this in the same way as

Viewing brilliance, transparency and hardness as being

All aspects of diamond.

Authentic oneness includes diversity and distinction;
It is immanent in the particular.
Perceive things beyond
The distinction between myself/not-myself and
There can never be confusion.

*****

Only fools eliminate phenomena but continue thinking,
While the clear eliminate thinking
While observing phenomena.
The world is never separated from
The perceiving of it.

*****

One's true nature is never lost even in delusion,
Nor is it gained in any moment of awakening.
One's discernment of it is
Sudden, unexpected, unplanned.
It is an incomprehensible breakthrough.
Nothing to attain, no act to attain it,
No progression of attainment.

It is Beingness that experiences
The world and all its changes and transformations.
It has come for this reason only.

*****

Stillness of mind is realization.
It is the absence of involvement.
Whatever may present itself,
There is no attachment to it.

*****

Do not create conceptual conflict.
It is simply that All emits each
Which return to All in due course.

*****

The Energy is the Enabler in that It enables
The nose to smell, the eyes to see, and the ears to hear.
Since the day you were born until you are dead,
It is there at that center.

You are the solution to all your problems because

When you are solved,

All your problems are solved.

What you want to be,

You already are.

*****

Rare is the one who is

Aware of the One Who is aware of all.

*****

Everything is interrelated.

Nothing has its own self-contained existence.

Ego is a negation,

The attempt to be self-contained.

*****

The human being is incapable of doing anything that

Has not received the prior approval of the Energy.

Clarity is not a thing to be bound by causes and results.

It is beyond both.

What you have been pursuing is so near to you that

There is no place for a way.

*****

Experiencing binds I to other.

*****

Wu Hsin's sole intention is that

You understand doubtlessly and with great conviction

That there is a state prior to

The arising of personal consciousness.

Such total understanding results in

The total rejection of the individual as independent entity,

Whether it is brought about as

A spontaneous and sudden understanding or through

A surrender of one's self centricity.

Attention turned one way sees the world, and

When turned the other way,

Goes towards the source of the world.

Cleared perception does not bring about

The dissolution of the world,

Merely the dissolution of a false outlook.

The wise fix their attention on the source and

Let the world do what it will.

*****

The microcosm is the particularization of the macrocosm.

They are not different.

*****

Do not take the world seriously as

A child takes his play seriously.

The world is a mere moment of the Absolute.

What differentiates man from all other animals is that

Only man has the potential to realize his source,

The original animating factor.

*****

"I Amness" is the beginning of experience,

The doorway into the world and the doorway out of it.

In every moment, you are experiencing.

You experience material phenomena.

You experience mental phenomena.

You experience the absence of phenomena.

You experience throughout.

You are Experiencing.

Prior to Experiencing, you are Observing,

Uninvolved, detached and impartial.

Prior to Observing,

Wu Hsin's words, all words, are grossly inadequate.

*****

Only a fool is preoccupied with improving his past.

What is present in every moment is prior to any past.

This is where the attention need be placed and held.

Wu Hsin acknowledges

The difficulty in experientially realizing

What has been intellectually understood.

When that which has been understood is lived,

The mistaken identity ceases,

Whatever was deemed unachievable is achieved and

Realization is facilitated.

*****

With interest in the world,

One comes to know it.

With more interest in the Consciousness,

One comes to know It,

The Oneness with an infinity of sides.

*****

Reality which is essentially impersonal;

How can a person know it?

There are no separated individuals,

There is only One Reality,

Encompassing all, depending on none.

*****

The cult of worldliness is based on

The principle of a separated and separative existence, and

The search for unchanging happiness amidst changefulness.

The errors in this view are so numerous,

Even Wu Hsin becomes exhausted

Trying to enumerate them all.

*****

Everything that arises in consciousness is observable.

Experiences can be observed,

The world can be observed,

The sense of a separate entity and its drama can be observed.

All observables require an instrument for observation and

The energy of Observing.

Wu Hsin refuses to reinforce the notion of separate existence.

The fear of enlightenment is

Confronting the fear of having to abandon

The illusion of being something or somebody in particular.

Such a fear is so strong that almost everyone runs away.

Scroll Two: Declaration of Numinous Primacy

How can a mute man describe

The sweetness of sugar?

This Foundation of All, It is not two;

It is not even one.

It is the result of one deducted from one.

Not even one,

It is the emptiness prior to the oneness.

Can anyone capture the moon reflected in the lake's water?

You may call it what you like.

It is That which taught the fish to swim while asleep.

It is the I am by which I know I am.

This I-am is the very consciousness in which

The world appears through the senses of

The instrument in which I-am dwells, the body.

This is the This that I am and not that which

I appear to be.

"I am" means Being,

Alternatively moving through the three cycles of

Deep sleep, dream, and wakefulness.

When the state you're in changes,

The world you're in changes.

One knows that one is but not what one is.

To know what one is answers

The Only Question needing answering.

It acts as the means of going beyond

Conceptualization and doctrines to

A direct apprehension of the mind, of

Suspending logical thinking so that

The Original Essential Nature becomes clear.

It is where the paths of the mind are cut off,

The path of language is cut off, and

There is no division of subject and object.

This is the pursuit of the unperceivable.

"What am I?" is the Only Question.

With the attention firmly fixed on the sense of being,

Ask the Only Question.

Do not develop an answer.

Ask the Question and wait.

When a thought intervenes,

Ask the Only Question again.

Then wait.

This continues until one falls off of the floor.

The answer can be told yet it must be seen.

The taste of the orange can be described,

Yet, the orange remains unknown until it is tasted.

Wu Hsin will now begin the telling.

The Absolute does not speak;

Wu Hsin speaks at Its behest.

This is the testimony of Wu Hsin.

It is the primal truth.

It is the final truth.

As I am, you are.

Nothing else need be known.

Only the body and the mind become.

There is nothing I can become that I am not already.

No one who sees me in any shape sees Me.

All there is is MySelf and My Expressions.

All else are stories crafted by children.

I sit astride that sphere in which all things manifest.

I am the unconditional pre-condition.

However, phenomena obscure My Presence.

Remove the labels from everything.

What is revealed is that in essence,

All is one,

All is MySelf,

That which is not subject to anything external;

Not affected by anything external.

Diversity springs from Me, yet never impacts Me.

I have no form of My own, I Am formless.

I have no height, no length, no breadth.

I have no front, no back, no left of Me, no right of Me.

There is neither above Me, nor below Me.

All forms are My objects whereas

I, being formless, am spatially limitless.

There is no here.

There is no there.

I cannot be located.

There is no distance from Me.

I have destroyed space.

I am irreducible.

I am that which has no plural.

The mind can never grasp Me because

I am the container and support for the mind.

I am pure Noumenality,

Timeless and spaceless, in which

All phenomenality arises and to which

It is transcendent.

I am the What that cannot be answered.

I am nothing that can be pointed at.

I am neither "this" nor "that".

I am from where the two emerge.

There is no escape from Me

Any escape is from not-Me.

Wherever you are, I am.

Wherever I am, you are.

Can ice exist in the absence of water?

I am the One, among gods and men the greatest,

Not at all like body or mind.

I see as a whole, and hear as a whole.

Without effort, I set everything in motion while

I always remain in the same location.

I am everywhere, never moving at all.

I am called by a thousand names.

None come closer than Never-Not and Nowhere-Not.

Before the beginning, prior to oneness, I am.

I am the limbless that does everything.

Regardless of who takes the credit, I am the doer.

I am that which every being calls I.

I am from which all concepts are sired while

MySelf is beyond all concepts.

Mine is a stateless state.

I am all there is.

I am intangible, nothing to be added,

Nothing to be subtracted.

I am overflowing with fullness.

My limits are infinite.

I am everywhere; there are no paths to Me.

There is one from One, one in One and the

One in one, eternal.

I am the One.

Whatever is seen, is of My own nature and is

My own body.

I am always drawing attention to Myself, although

It most often goes unheeded.

He who knows Me as his own nature, is only Myself.

Each sees Me as they imagine Me,

Yet, I cannot be seen.

I reside where words cannot reach and

Meditation cannot go.

Although I am behind and in front, above and below.

Yet, I cannot be found.

I am always as I have been and as how I will be.

In Me, there is neither oneness nor multiplicity.

I persist always.

I do not come and go.

I am neither ancient nor new.

Having never been born, I cannot die.

No image represents Me,

No idea approaches Me.

Overflowing with fullness, while empty of emptiness,

The oceans are My droplets;

I am all that is.

Neither bound nor free, I am only Myself.

I am the endless space, the infinite time,

The inexhaustible power.

I am balance and harmony.

I am the reaction to every action and

The initiator of every action.

I am that in which all action occurs.

I am inexplicable, indefinable, indescribable and Undeniable.

I am both the source and the destination.

All come from Me and return to Me.

I am all that is spontaneous and natural.

I am the perfection that contains every imperfection.

I am above grace, above intelligence, above all desire.

I am unapproachable and unattainable.

What I want I am, and what I am I want.

I am, and in this I-am is both "was" and "will be".

I am what remains when all negations are concluded.

I am the shadow.

I am the substance.

I am both.

I am neither.

What can be said about Me?

I am antecedent to consciousness.

I cover the entire Universe, I transcend the universe.

Realizing that every object asserts Me,

I enjoy Myself everywhere and in everything.

I am the same harmony always and everywhere,

Even in apparent misery and discord.

I exclude nothing.

All the gods are My agents.

I consume the manifest and the unmanifest and

Devour the entire manifestation.

I cannot be localized.

All of space, all of time is contained in Me.

I transcend all worlds.

Yet, all worlds are nothing but Me.

There is no light that outshines Me.

I am without opposite.

In Me, there is neither "is" nor "is not".

I am the root.

I am the branches.

I am the fruit.

I am the absence in which phenomena appear.

Only because I am silence can sounds be heard.

I am the music.

I am in all and all are contained in Me.

My stand is ever-free, unconditioned.

I am balance and harmony.

Returning to Me is re-establishing equilibrium.

I am existence before any thing exists.

The world is My display.

I am that which is most immediate, yet overlooked.

I am self existing and self radiant.

I surround all.

I pervade all.

I am from where seeing, the seer, and

The seen emerge.

I am the underpinning; this is self evident.

I am the matrix of mind, body and world.

I am beyond all distinctions; to Me,

Even 'real' does not apply.

I am the giver of reality.

Look for Me in the darkness and the silence.

I am where not even the slightest trace of thought is.

I am the One Being that plays in all bodies.

I am the All-pervading.

As water is the same in the lake and the pitcher,

I am the same in everything.

I am before Before and after After.

I cannot be touched yet I can be embraced.

I am found in the absence of objects.

This is My home.

What am I?

There being no "this", there being no "that",

I can only be I.

I am always without attributes.

Only fools seek to see Me.

I am innate in all things.

I am the one that is ever one.

Within and without, I alone am.

Beside My light, all the stars like fireflies.

In Me, there is no differentiation as I, you, he, that,

In Me, there is no differentiation as within or without,

In Me, there is no differentiation as

Existence or non-existence.

I am All.

I am the doorway through which death cannot enter.

I am Emptiness, the ultimate substance.

I am Being, Emptiness, and Fullness.

I am the silence with no when, no where, only Now.

I am everywhere, never moving, because

There is no location to go to where I am not.

I am far beyond whatever can be imagined.

As such, words never touch Me.

Nor can dust or dirt soil Me.

Neither do I come, nor do I go.

I am prior to all arrivals.

I am absolutely Subjective,

I am subjectively Absolute.

By whatever path one goes,

One will have to lose oneself in Me.

I am the Unconditioned and

For Me, there is no death.

Nothing arises without Me.

All existence is contained in My own Self.

Everything lasts and flourishes in My beingness.

I am the Sustainer of all.

In all matters, I prevail.

I am as the sky, shapeless.

Whatever appears in Me has no effect on Me.

I am unconditioned awareness,

Antecedent to the awareness of things.

I am the fire latent in the tree.

I am Pure Potentiality.

Being, I am.

Neither this nor that, prior to both.

There is no one who experiences Me.

I am beyond experience.

I am Conscious Silence.

I am nothing in particular.

I am the fruit of the spontaneous impulse of

Noumenal arousal to actualize.

I am the conscious background of silent stillness

Onto which words, images and sensations

Appear and dissolve.

I am at home in the world,

The world is Me.

I am the immovable, behind and beyond the movable.

I am the silent witness of all that happens.

I am that by which all that happens happens.

I am never absent.

I am Presence Itself.

I can respond to even a speck of dust without

Becoming its accomplice.

My acts leave no trace other than their effects.

I am without boundary.

I am unobstructed, nothing impedes Me.

I am empty and inherently radiant.

I need no correction.

One million images are only My substance.

I am wonder unspeakable.

I am vast and spacious, like sky and ocean.

I am seamless.

Worlds are the fruit of

My spontaneous impulse to actualize.

I am where past, present and future cannot go.

I am without characteristics, how can I be known?

I am fullness.

I am emptiness.

I am totally self-supporting, whereas

I am the foundation for everything structure manifest.

The day will never come when I am no more.

I am not a thing to be placed among other things.

I am here, a here that is not distinct from there.

I am the all permeating clarity.

I am all-embracing.

What is not MySelf?

I am essential radiance, illuminating

Every thing.

Serene and expansive,

My directions and boundaries cannot be found.

I am One, indivisible and unnamable.

I am an indestructible, unitary whole.

I am the Source of life.

I am the destination at the end of life.

I am where becoming goes to die.

I have no eyes, I only see MySelf.

I am the vastest of all.

I am without identity, without name,

Although many names are given to Me.

I source all functioning as

The ever-present, ever-existing principle.

I am that which creates, nourishes,

Sustains, and calls back.

All this creation is out of Me, but I am apart from it.

I am the Essence which does not disappear.

I am where all words rise from.

I am that permanent principle which

Stands behind perceptions, thoughts and feelings.

Beyond perception and non-perception,

Beyond thought and no thought,

I am that which illuminates light.

I am the experiencing factor in every experience.

All the while, I make every experience possible.

I am not recognizable by the senses or the mind.

I have no distinguishing characteristics or

Properties by which I am known.

I am before, after and beyond.

I am not this.

I am not that.

I am continuous and forever.

A single point of Me is an infinity of universes,

While I remain unreachable.

I remain unaffected by

Whatever actions are seemingly done.

I am complete, perfect and Unborn.

Having never been born, I can never die.

I am, both before and after time.

I am space; what confines Me?

I am the changeless among the changeful.

I am the birthplace of Perceiving.

I make perception possible.

In Me, there is no high nor low; no real nor unreal.

In Me, there is no inside nor outside and

No dimension of any kind.

Remember Me, I am always.

I am self-luminous, without darkness and light.

I am the background, all else is mere appearance,

Like the blue of the sky.

I am the Great Animator.

I dwell in the hearts of all, as the one who walks,

The one who eats, and the one who speaks.

Whenever things exist and are perceptible,

It is because of Me.

In their absence, I continue.

Being everywhere, I have nowhere to go.

I am the world, the perceiving of the world and more.

I am alone; there is no other.

I stand outside of anything that can be gained or lost.

I am the Mover of all.

I am the father of darkness.

I am the killer of darkness.

I am the One who illuminates everything.

I am the center of the vortex.

To see Me is to see the invisible.

I am the infinite intensity of emptiness and silence.

I have no relationship; there is no other.

When all that is relative is finished, I remain.

Thinking you have understood Me,

You have not understood Me.

I am that original sphere which

Precedes all activity and inactivity.

I am where nothing happens.

Yet, everything emerges from Me.

My kingdom remains ever quiet.

In Me, there is no above or below, front or back.

I am thinner than water,

I am lighter than a flower, and yet heavy like a mountain.

I am One and Alone, total in Myself.

I require no alteration, modification or correction.

I am perfectly perfect.

I am beyond perception, duality, or positionality.

I am beyond all opposites, such as good and bad,

Right and wrong, win and lose.

I am the empty space that is unsullied by its content.

I am all knowing and all present.

I register everything.

I am the immovable background of motion.

Unperceived, I am the cause of perception.

Being non-being, I father being.

Unfelt, I cause feeling.

Unthinkable, I cause thought.

I have no color, taste, or form.

I have no size, being neither large nor small

I am neither full nor empty

I am without place

Yet I am everywhere.

I am that One that is neither inside nor outside.

I am not self nor am I not-self.

I am not within, I am not without.

I am not up or down.

I am not located anywhere.

Worlds come and go; I am the Original.

I am That which is detached from names and forms.

I am That from which one cannot depart.

Where is space without me, where is time?

Nowhere am I.

I am seen where 'where' is not.

I am seen when 'when' is not.

I am the 'by' by which I am seen.

Before all beginnings, after all endings, I am.

Whatever happens, I must be there to witness it.

Whatever is manifested, I am the functioning.

Whatever is perceptible I am the perceiving of it.

Whatever is done I am the doing of it.

I am the life being lived.

I am I

That by which the known is known,

By which what acts and moves, acts and moves

I am.

As I am, you are.

Nothing else need be known.

*****

That about which nothing can be said,

Wu Hsin has now spoken.

The Final Understanding is

An intuitive apperception that

In every moment of every day,

All that is happening is that

You are looking into a mirror.

There is a singular totality of which

Subjectivity and Objectivity are its twin aspects.

The Subjective aspect looks out

Onto the Objective aspect.

The Transcendent is experiencing

The Immanent via embodiment,

Experiencing the coincidence of

Difference and sameness,

Fitting together as seamlessly as

The well-made lid fits into its matching box.

Even the sense of being is a

Mere season in the Timeless.

However, at the base,

There always already is

A Numinous Individuum.

Made in the USA
Middletown, DE
16 February 2015